B♭ CLARINET

Sounds of Celebration

Solos with Ensemble Arrangements for Two or More Players

Arranged by Stan Pethel

CONTENTS

DIGITAL DOWNLOAD CODE
To access audio MP3 files, go to:
www.halleonard.com/mylibrary

Enter Code
4806-5657-5359-5649

Daybreak MUSIC
EXCLUSIVELY DISTRIBUTED BY
HAL•LEONARD

As the Deer
(with "My Faith Looks Up to Thee")

B♭ CLARINET
Solo

Words and Music by **MARTIN NYSTROM**
Arranged by **STAN PETHEL**

As the Deer

(with "My Faith Looks Up to Thee")

B♭ CLARINET
Ensemble

Words and Music by **MARTIN NYSTROM**
Arranged by **STAN PETHEL**

Give Thanks
(with "Now Thank We All Our God")

B♭ CLARINET
Solo

Words and Music by **HENRY SMITH**
Arranged by **STAN PETHEL**

NOW THANK WE ALL OUR GOD
German Words by MARTIN RINKART, English Translation by CATHERINE WINKWORTH
Music by JOHANN CRÜGER

Give Thanks
(with "Now Thank We All Our God")

B♭ CLARINET
Ensemble

Words and Music by **HENRY SMITH**
Arranged by **STAN PETHEL**

Glorify Thy Name
(with "We Will Glorify")

B♭ CLARINET
Solo

Words and Music by **DONNA ADKINS**
Arranged by **STAN PETHEL**

Glorify Thy Name
(with "We Will Glorify")

B♭ CLARINET
Ensemble

Words and Music by **DONNA ADKINS**
Arranged by **STAN PETHEL**

Great Is the Lord

B♭ CLARINET
Solo

Words and Music by **MICHAEL W. SMITH**
and **DEBORAH D. SMITH**
Arranged by **STAN PETHEL**

Great Is the Lord

B♭ CLARINET
Ensemble

Words and Music by **MICHAEL W. SMITH**
and **DEBORAH D. SMITH**
Arranged by **STAN PETHEL**

With energy (♩ = *ca.* 76)

He Is Exalted

(with "O For a Thousand Tongues to Sing")

B♭ CLARINET
Solo

Words and Music by **TWILA PARIS**
Arranged by **STAN PETHEL**

He Is Exalted

(with "O For a Thousand Tongues to Sing")

B♭ CLARINET
Ensemble

Words and Music by **TWILA PARIS**
Arranged by **STAN PETHEL**

I Love You Lord
(with "My Jesus, I Love Thee")

B♭ CLARINET
Solo

Words and Music by **LAURIE KLEIN**
Arranged by **STAN PETHEL**

I Love You Lord

(with "My Jesus, I Love Thee")

B♭ CLARINET
Ensemble

Words and Music by **LAURIE KLEIN**
Arranged by **STAN PETHEL**

Lord, I Lift Your Name on High

(with "All Hail the Power of Jesus' Name")

B♭ CLARINET
Solo

Words and Music by **RICK FOUNDS**
Arranged by **STAN PETHEL**

LORD, I LIFT YOUR NAME ON HIGH

ALL HAIL THE POWER OF JESUS' NAME

Lord, I Lift Your Name on High

(with "All Hail the Power of Jesus' Name")

B♭ CLARINET
Ensemble

Words and Music by **RICK FOUNDS**
Arranged by **STAN PETHEL**

More Precious than Silver

(with "When I Survey the Wondrous Cross")

B♭ CLARINET
Solo

Words and Music by **LYNN DESHAZO**
Arranged by **STAN PETHEL**

More Precious than Silver

(with "When I Survey the Wondrous Cross")

B♭ CLARINET
Ensemble

Words and Music by **LYNN DESHAZO**
Arranged by **STAN PETHEL**

Not too fast, with expression (♩ = *ca.* 108)

Shine, Jesus, Shine

Words and Music by **GRAHAM KENDRICK**
Arranged by **STAN PETHEL**

B♭ CLARINET
Solo

Shine, Jesus, Shine

B♭ CLARINET
Ensemble

Words and Music by **GRAHAM KENDRICK**
Arranged by **STAN PETHEL**

Shout to the Lord

B♭ CLARINET
Solo

Words and Music by DARLENE ZSCHECH
Arranged by STAN PETHEL

37
legato
mp
42
45
47
51
53 more accented
f
55
59
61
63
67
71
ff
rit.

Shout to the Lord

B♭ CLARINET
Ensemble

Words and Music by **DARLENE ZSCHECH**
Arranged by **STAN PETHEL**

37
42
45
47
51
53
as before
f
55
59
61
62
65
67
69
ff
73
rit.